for Alex, the mind
for John, the courage
for Kari, the heart

for my family, "There ain't no place like home."

Old Shirts & New Skins

by Sherman Alexie

with illustrations by Elizabeth Woody

American Indian Studies Center
University of California, Los Angeles
3220 Campbell Hall
Los Angeles, California 90024-1548

NATIVE AMERICAN SERIES NO. 9

Books in this series are published for the purpose of encouraging American Indian authorship in expressive literature.

Editor: Kenneth Lincoln, English Department, UCLA
Publications Editor: Duane Champagne, Sociology Department, UCLA
Managing Editor: Judith St. George

ACKNOWLEDGMENTS

Some of the poems in this book have been published or will appear in *Another Chicago Magazine, Beloit Poetry Journal, Black Bear Review, Caliban, Deep Down Things, Jacaranda Review, Journal of Ethnic Studies, Kenyon Review, Lactuca, Mr. Cogito, North Dakota Quarterly, NRG, Red Dirt, Slipstream, Z Miscellaneous, and ZYZZYVA.*

Cover: "Blue Woman Potter," by Elizabeth Woody

Printed by Pace Publication Arts, Anaheim, California

Hearty thanks to Brian Swann for the gift of royalties from *Smoothing the Ground* to help publish this book.

Library of Congress Catalog Card No. 92-53282
ISBN No. 0-935626-36-0
© 1993 The Regents of the University of California

American Indian Studies Center
University of California
Los Angeles, California
USA

Foreword

INDIAN EDUCATION

SONGS FROM THE FILM

DROUGHT

FOREWORD

"While American Indians have a grand past, their impact on the culture of the world has been slight. There are no great American Indian novels, no poetry, no memorable music. Their totem pole does not rank with the statuary of Greece and there is no American Indian art except for some good craft works in wool, pottery, and silver." Not long ago, Andy Rooney, the aging, self-appointed humorist of the television program *60 Minutes,* wrote these deprecating and racist words in his nationally syndicated column. While the words from this potato-headed pontiff may seem off the wall and innocuous to some, they drew the ire of Indian people across the country. Perhaps Rooney, in the steel and concrete valleys of Manhattan, had never heard the names of the brilliant Indian poets who are writing today like Joy Harjo, Luci Tapahonso, and Simon Ortiz. I don't think I could name but a few Irish-American poets, but I find it hard to believe he has never heard of the novelists D'Arcy McNickle, Scott Momaday, James Welch, Louise Erdrich, and so on.

The point I want to make of this is that Indian people are still a largely invisible race. For most Americans, we are perceived to be extinct, or something distant and related to the sometimes romantic, sometimes halting caricatures on the silver screen. The truth is, sadly, that very few of our Indian writers speak to the condition of the majority of our Indian people. There is only a very small handful of writers who speak directly for those Indians living in Indian communities on Indian land—the enrolled members of federally recognized tribes. It is not my intent here to replicate the litany of oppressed whining that we often fall into, but to make concrete who and what we are as Indians. For the most part, we are a disenfranchised people whose lands, cultures, and very voices have been stolen, used, and abused. A good many of us are as dependent now on federal handouts for our very survival as we were when we were first caged in reservations in the late nineteenth century. We seem to burn furiously towards our own self-destruction, and yet we survive, we will always survive. Despite the occasional glimmer of bright spots, and occasional hope and success for some of us, the future looks extremely harsh and discouraging for most of us, and yet we continue to survive in that ever-widening chasm between the old ways and today. Sherman Alexie speaks in a voice that contains ancient wisdom and the fresh spontaneity of today's youth. He knows who we are and what we were before we crossed the land bridge in the Bering Straits on our way down to Haskell Indian School.

It is so important for us when a poet like Sherman Alexie emerges to detail our dreams, our hopes, and our embattled states of being. He fulfills the traditional decrees of poetry: He speaks to people in hopes of bringing about change; he speaks as a functioning ear and eye of the people; he speaks as a seer. Alexie is not writing the intellectualized masturbation that passes for so much of today's poetry. He is a singer, a shaman, a healer, a virtual Freddy Fender saying, "Hey baby, *que paso?* I thought I was your only *vato.*"

When a visionary writer like Sherman Alexie comes along, there is a brief freshening of air upon our bleak and stagnant landscape. In the parlance of today's reservation, we immediately perceive him to be a "skin," a brother we can trust. He speaks of how we truly live and how we truly feel. There are so many "Native American" writers who are unable to do this, and because Alexie can and does it in passionate brilliance, he is immediately propelled to the front rank of Indian writers now writing. He speaks for all who have been marginalized, whose voices have been silenced by oppression and racism. He speaks for us. He is us.

It has been said that a Native American "literary renaissance" is upon us, and judging by the spate of recent books by "Native Americans," something is happening. This phenomenon is exciting and good, but also bad because a number of those writers now publishing books would be hard pressed to prove membership in a federally recognized Indian tribe. Moreover, many of them prove their ignorance of the real Indian world with their writings. Some are *poseurs,* others are "culture vultures" who somehow magically became Indian. Others are merely descendants of Indian ancestors and know little of American Indian life today except what they have read in books; they can "talk the talk," but they can't "walk the walk." This "renaissance" is a grab bag of the real and the surreal, abounding with outright fakes, romantic academics, and liberal anthropologist types. Sherman Alexie is none of the above. He is the real deal and quite a gifted one at that, a poet who knows the fine joys and madnesses brought on by cheap wine and commodity foods, poverty and alienation, our irrepressible sense of humor and the serenade of the Indian drums and Indian songs.

Sherman Alexie is young, in his twenties, and is an enrolled Spokane/Coeur D'Alene Indian from Wellpinit, on the Spokane Indian Reservation of Washington. *Old Shirts & New Skins* is his third published book of poems this year. His first remarkable collection of poems and stories, *The Business of Fancydancing*, was published in New York this spring and was quickly followed by his chapbook, *I Would Steal Horses*. In this year, Alexie has virtually exploded upon the Indian literary scene. His poems have appeared in numerous reviews and journals, including prestigious ones like the *Kenyon Review*, the *North Dakota Quarterly*, and the *New York Quarterly*. He is the brightest star in the younger constellation of American Indian writers, and I predict in a few short years he will be regarded as one of the leading voices of those who write and speak for Indian people. Our premier Indian poet, Joy Harjo, has said of Alexie, "He is a compassionate trickster who travels the page carrying an amazing bag of tricks. Watch this guy. He's making myth." And he is. He does!

Old Shirts & New Skins is a dazzling trip through the mind of a brilliant young poet and fiction writer. Filled with poems that can make you laugh and cry, this book is neither strident nor self-pitying. It is remarkable in its candor, and gracefully constructed. Choreographed with those objects and events that construct American Indian life today, these poems bind us to the present, yet at the same time connect us to the ancestral voices of our past. In the forlorn saloons, on the gym floors of the Six-foot and under basketball tournaments, among the stacks of commodity foods in HUD houses, lost in cities, or at powwows, we still hear the whispers of Crazy Horse. Beyond the bright and brilliant costumes of the fancydancer, we see the earth-toned permutations of our traditional ways. We are tethered like dog soldiers to Indian land and to the reservation of the spirit and the mind.

Many of the poems in this collection turn on an axis of irony, and, as a consequence, the reader may view Alexie himself as a trickster figure telling stories. The stories he tells inside these poems are wondrous. His language is clear and concise and not intellectualized to the point of losing the reader. *Old Shirts & New Skins* is a book that will be very much appreciated by Indian writers, scholars, and students. This book, like his first collection, *The Business of Fancydancing*, is very accessible to Indian college students, a fact that I know firsthand. Again and again my students repeated one simple comment which can at the same time be regarded as the highest form of compliment: "This guy knows what he's talking about. He knows the real Indian world." It is my belief that *Old Shirts & New Skins* is a book that Indians can relate to because it was not written for the white literary establishment and yet at the same time is powerful literature. Surely Sherman Alexie does not need me to pimp for him, but I must say that what follows is a book of urgent and extreme power and elegant poetic vision. Read on. Read on and enjoy, feel, and learn what it is to be Indian in the twentieth century of this mad and careless nation. Read on and taste the soul of the Indian and hear the drum, which is not the sound of the heart, but the booming of thunder.

Adrian C. Louis
Pine Ridge, South Dakota

INDIAN EDUCATION

Poetry = Anger x Imagination
—Lester FallsApart

INTRODUCTION TO
NATIVE AMERICAN LITERATURE

*Isn't it enough that I give you my life
to mess around with that I must give you
the last words to the story too?*
— Alex Kuo

Somewhere in America a television explodes

& here you are again (again)
asking me to explain broken glass.

You scour the reservation landfill
through the debris of so many lives:
old guitar, basketball on fire, pair of shoes.
All you bring me is an empty bottle.

Am I the garbageman of your dreams?

*

Listen:

it will not save you
or talk you down from the ledge
of a personal building.

It will not kill you
or throw you facedown to the floor
& pull the trigger twice.

It believes a roomful of monkeys
in a roomful of typewriters
would eventually produce a roomful
of poetry about missing the jungle.

You will forget
more than you remember:
that is why we all dream slowly.

Often, you need change of scenery.
It will give you one black & white photograph.

Sometimes, it whispers
into anonymous corner bars
& talks too much about the color
of its eyes & skin & hair.

It believes a piece of coal
shoved up its own ass
will emerge years later
as a perfectly imperfect diamond.

Sometimes, it screams
the English language near freeways
until trucks jackknife & stop all traffic
while the city runs over itself.

Often, you ask forgiveness.
It will give you a 10% discount.

*

Because you have seen the color of my bare skin
does not mean you have memorized the shape of my ribcage.

Because you have seen the spine of the mountain
does not mean you made the climb.

Because you stood waist-deep in the changing river
does not mean you were equal to MC^2.

Because you gave something a name
does not mean your name is important.

Because you sleep
does not mean you see into my dreams.

*

Send it a letter: the address will keep changing.
Give it a phone call: busy signal.
Knock on its door: you'll hear voices.

Look in its windows: shadows dance through the blinds.

In the end, it will pick you up from the pavement
& take you to the tribal cafe for breakfast.

It will read you the menu.
It will not pay your half of the bill.

ANTHROPOLOGY

Their bones are so sharp they can break through their own excuses.
— Jim Carroll

In the Indian Health Service Clinic, the doctor tells me the cancer has spread into my eyes, will steal my vision, but it hasn't grown into my bones.

"You must remember," he whispers. "You will be remembered by the shape of your femur, fibula, scapula."

Then, I cut my skin into sixteen equal pieces, keep thirteen buried in my backyard and feed the other three to the dogs.

I am left with my bones, the X-rays of my expectations.

The leg bones staggering home from the powwow grounds, carrying the weight of ten thousand dreams down a basketball court, bending deep at the knee just before the fall.

The arm bones reaching across the stick game, holding up the thumb on every highway leading off the reservation, bending at the elbow to hold the hydrocephalic head off the table.

The endless ribcage, each curved bone like a story, split open in the dust of another century; each curved bone like a promise, picked clean and waiting for identification.

The skull, cup of sharing, filled with old water, alcohol, spit from toothless mouths, all tasting so familiar.

Then and before, my face in the morning mirror, small bones breaking through brown skin, my brother behind me, burning flashbulb after flashbulb, filling a roll of film. The black and white photographs hidden between the pages of dictionaries, stuffed into the pockets of old coats, taped to the walls and painted over, secreted into the crawlspace of a HUD house.

Evidence, evidence.

Now, in the dark of the house near Benjamin Lake, I hear digging, the slow moan of earth changing, the silence of something taken, cold wind rushing in to fill the empty spaces.

ARCHITECTURE

The reservation is full of these rooms
where four walls make a home. Foot by foot,
we measure definitions

assigned to us by years. We draw lines
bisecting what never changes and what does
is the distance between
touching and becoming. There are promises

we can map across landscape
of our body, becoming more of what matters
in a house without doors or windows,

where hands are the weapon, pressed
tightly against its heartbeat, breaking us
down into everything we want to own.

ECONOMICS OF THE TRIBE

after James Welch

solvent means having enough money
to get drunk in Springdale again
means the checks came in
money is free if you're poor enough
most times we are

saving means putting money away
for the weekend or powwow

bond means you're in jail
only interest you can get
is an interest in getting out

finance don't mean nothing
because that is just money
money all over the place money
tucked in our wallets and shoes

risk don't mean stock market
means we risk cash playing
poker or the stickgame means
carrying it all in our pockets
passing out at powwow

PHYSICAL EDUCATION

Sundays, when I was young, my father
and I
played basketball. On those days
Eugene
was sober, he borrowed an old
pair of shoes and

never missed from the corner. He and
my father
stole from each other's lungs, growing old
while I
remained Little Man, in town hat and hair. Eugene
measured his days

against mine, like the spaces between bones, my days
growing and
reaching past the calendars Eugene
and my father
carried in their livers, blackened by whiskey and, I
thought, the old

memories of missed free throws, memories of the old
days
when an Indian basketball player could be Jesus. I
grew and
knew it was *Damn* and *Goddamn* when my father
and Eugene

leaned into the key, their bodies, against time, Eugene
a step old
and fifteen years younger than my father.
On most days,
my father had more from the night before, and
Eugene and I

both knew it, felt it in the hands, and I
watched Eugene
move out of himself then, a piece at a time, and
like an old
house on fire, I wanted to rescue those days
from the ash, my father,

who lived and only grew old
while I watched Eugene die and
forgive all the days he forgave my father.

FORESTRY

Monday morning it had to be when we, meaning the three of us, as in Joe-Joe, Stan and me, cutting through brush thick as our hungover vision when Stan cut the hornet nest in half.

There was no time for fear, our stomachs throw-up empty, our spirit animals chased us back to the truck like ironic arrows.

I was the bravest warrior, killed many hornets while stung only twelve times. Joe-Joe was in the hospital for a week. Stan ran past the truck that day, is still running, slapping his skin, waving his arms wildly at real and imagined enemies.

Late at night, you can hear Stan's song echo across the reservation, his feet pounding the earth like a drum.

It is the loneliest song you will ever hear.

LEARNING TO DROWN

*Hydrocephalus: an abnormal increase in the
amount of cerebrospinal fluid within the
cranial cavity that is accompanied by expansion
of the cerebral ventricles, enlargement of the skull
and especially, the forehead, and atrophy of the brain.*
— Webster's Ninth New Collegiate Dictionary

1.
Driving all night, I hear a story
on the radio about prisoners
of war in some foreign country.

Their captors had no room left
to house them, nearly 600 men,
so they marched them down

to a nearby river
and drowned all of them,
one by one, while the other

prisoners watched
from the river bank, silent,
bowed into themselves.

2.
"Water on the brain"
makes the definition easier
to understand, anticipates

the questions always asked:
"What kind of dreams did you have?"
"Was it like drowning?"

I can still see my reflection
in water, my face
flooding the banks, a body

of water erasing boundaries,
changing the distance
between past and present.

3.
I remember the reservation girl
with Down's Syndrome,
weighing over 300 pounds,

wading in Benjamin Lake,
feet tangled in weeds,
falling facedown

into six inches of water.
My cousin, ten years old,
trying to lift her,

trying to turn her over,
trying anything
to make her breathe.

4.
My mother tells me
the doctors would not believe
my skull was growing,

swelling, until my cousin
dropped me from a swing.
My mother tells me

I measured
the size of your head every day,
it grew an inch in one week,

but the doctors said no,
it was a mother's imagination
growing. I had nightmares

you were pressed against walls
of our house, breaking through,
that it would never stop.

5.

I used to go with my big brother
to a place on the Spokane River
where he and his friends

dared each other to swim
all the way across the water
to the opposite shore.

I would watch them,
some too scared to swim
past the shallow

water, most making it halfway
and coming back, coughing
water, a few struggling

in the middle
of the river, treading
water, my brother

swimming beyond sight.
I remember watching
water. I remember

waiting for my brother,
wanting to follow him
and recover myself again.

THE NAMING OF INDIAN BOYS

Sam Boyd disappeared
in San Francisco, years
before I was born, leaving
two brothers and one-third share
in a uranium mine
no one ever bothered to name.

Jesse Mathews gave his name
to a son before he disappeared.
"This child is mine,"
he must have said, years
ago, unwilling to share
that part of himself, leaving

his wife with an absence, leaving
a son with absence for a name.
Who are these men Indian boys share,
common heroes who disappeared
before we had blankets and years
to shelter them? Can I call them mine?

Can I call anything mine?
Did Sam Boyd, before leaving
the reservation all those years
ago, give everything away? Did he name
the possessions that appeared
in his hands, did he share

his name, will his share
of the uranium mine
to whoever appeared
at his door as he was leaving?
Did Jesse Mathews name
me, name every Indian boy? Year

after year after year,
do Indian boys share
a common, silent name?

Anonymously, has mine
been assigned to those leaving,
others who disappeared?

Do I give away what is mine, leaving
nothing unshared, for the disappeared
to return, years later, wearing my name?

GEOMETRY

Mornings, I measure the length and width of my basement bedroom in the HUD house. Like most on the reservation, our house is unfinished, and I'm worried that something will change while I sleep.

The ceremony is the same: I wake, shower, comb my hair into braids, take my tape measure from its hiding place and work quietly and quickly.

The tape measure I stole from the BIA, its maximum length is 12 feet and I worry the reservation will become smaller every time inventory is taken.

I have seen no evidence of that.

This morning, I found the wall facing the sunrise had grown half an inch during the night. I measured, remeasured, found the growth to be true and accurate.

I would not be telling you this unless I was even more surprised when I could not fit my feet into my shoes, and made silent when my father tore down the garage trying to squeeze our infinitely blue van out the door.

This is happening, you know.

INDIAN EDUCATION

Crazy Horse came back to life
in a storage room of the Smithsonian,
his body rising from a wooden crate
mistakenly marked ANONYMOUS HOPI MALE.

Crazy Horse wandered the halls, found
the surface of the moon, Judy Garland
and her red shoes, a stuffed horse named
Comanche, the only surviving

member of the Seventh Cavalry
at Little Big Horn. Crazy Horse was found
in the morning by a security guard
who took him home and left him alone

in a room with cable television. Crazy Horse
watched a basketball game, every black and white
western, a documentary about a scientist
who travelled the Great Plains in the 1800s

measuring Indians and settlers, discovering
that the Indians were two inches taller
on average, and in some areas, the difference
in height exceeded a foot, which proved nothing

although Crazy Horse measured himself
against the fact of a mirror, traded faces
with a taxi driver and memorized the city,
folding, unfolding, his mapped heart.

ARCHAEOLOGY

Beginning at that river
where spring floods uncovered

the long forgotten
burial ground of some tribe

or another, I search
for skulls and extra ribs

in the past. My hands reach
down, an exact process

into water, my own
reflection, and what it changes

I recognize. A shovel-shaped incisor
is all I need

to prove mouth
and face, eyes

set free, down river
to float nameless and see.

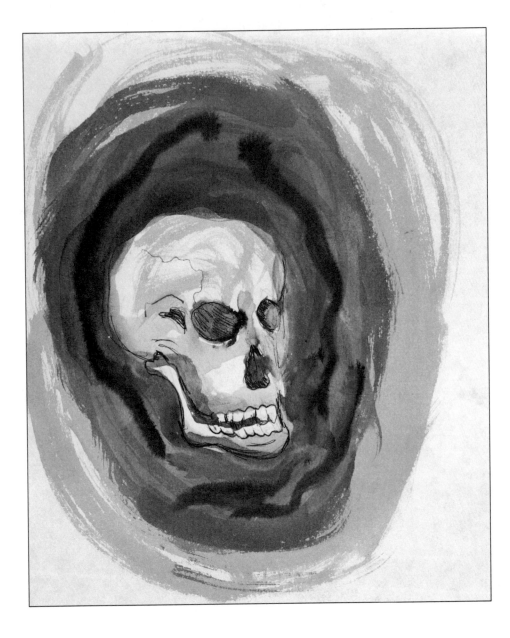

THE POSSIBILITIES OF
AGRICULTURE IN IDAHO

1.
authorities reported
an Indian girl

hitchhiking
between

Coeur d'Alene & Boise
disappeared

authorities reported
her backpack

found
in a wheatfield

five miles back
from the highway

indicated
signs of a struggle

authorities reported
no witnesses

2.
the farmer
climbing down

from his combine
touching

skull & spine
falling

in love
with what remains

red flannel shirt
blue jeans

her voice
promising

flesh
distant fields

all hoping
for fierce moments

of recognition
names

3.
acre after acre
disappears

they can break
your heart

NATURE POEM

If you're an Indian, why don't you write nature poetry?

inside this bottle
stands of pine
burning

Indian fire fighters
black ash faces
& 16 hour days

caught in the middle
ring of fire
they dug a hole

& burrowed in
pretending to be roots
or gophers, etc.

hoping the fires
would pass over
like an (eagle)

no one in the hole
was burned
fire sucked the air

from their lungs
buried in graves
they dug for themselves

SOCIOLOGY

Waiting in line for U. S. Commodities
I fell in love
with an Indian woman and her six kids

loading up a truck
with the maximum allowance.
I took her hand
and helped her into the cab

and drove them home
where my minimum wage
raised the household income
and lowered our benefits.

When the cheese was gone
she told me to leave.

OLD AND NEW TESTAMENT

Sitting in the Breakaway Bar with my third beer
when the Bible Man comes in, Wednesdays like usual,
and sits beside me with his double whiskey
and his "How do you do?" and "Brother,
are you saved?" He leaves at closing time
and I follow him, follow his tracks in the snow,
getting smaller and smaller with every block
until I look up and it's suddenly 4 a. m.
and the streetlights are flashing red,
red, red, red, my breath forming questions

out of the air. It takes me hours to find my way
back to my one room apartment in the Petticourt
where I soak my bluish feet in a basin of hot water,
peeling the skin off my soles.
Believing in everything I own, I stand at the window
watching one city block turning into another,
into another, into another, forgiving
everything I see, forgiving my inadequate god.

VISION (2)

No money for lunch so I rode an elevator to the top of the ONB Building, highest elevation in Spokane, where I stood at a window and witnessed 500 years of America: *Over 1 Billion Illusions Served.*

There is so much of this country I love, its supermarkets and bad television, the insane demands of a dollar bill in my pocket, fireworks celebrating the smallest occasions.

I am happy I can find a cup of hot coffee 24 hours a day.

But, America, in *my* country, there are no supermarkets and television is a way of never opening the front door. The fields here are green and there are no monuments celebrating the invasion of Christopher Columbus.

Here, I imagine 1492 and 1992 are two snakes entwined, climbing up the pole some call good medicine, while others name it progress or Manifest Destiny. Maybe it's economics or an extra-inning baseball game. Maybe it's Cotton Mather and Andrew Jackson looking for rescue. Maybe it's a smallpox blanket wrapped around our shoulders in the coldest winter.

Then again, who am I to talk? In the local newspaper I read this morning that my tribe escaped many of the hardships other Native Americans suffered. By the time the 20th century reached this far west, the war was over. Crazy Horse was gone and the Ghost Dancers were only ghosts. Christopher Columbus was 500 years and 3,000 miles away, fresh from a starring role in the Great American Movie.

I've seen that film at the reservation drive-in. If you look closely, you can see an Indian leaning against the back wall. You won't find his name among the end credits; you can't hear his voice or his song.

Extras, we're all extras.

HORSES

1,000 ponies, the United States Cavalry stole 1,000 ponies
from the Spokane Indians, shot 1,000 ponies & only 1 survived,
shot 1,000 ponies & left them as monuments, left 1,000 ponies
falling into dust, fallen, shot 1,000 ponies & only 1 survived.

*

At the last Spokane Tribal All-Indian Rodeo, I remember an Indian
cowboy, I remember an Indian cowboy rode a horse through a fence,
I remember an Indian cowboy rode a horse named Custer's Revenge,
the horse named Custer's Revenge broke through a fence, broke

through four-by-six-boards, after the bell, the horse broke through
a fence, I remember the Indian cowboy was thrown into the air,
I remember the horse named Custer's Revenge threw the Indian cowboy,
after the bell, the Indian cowboy was thrown into the air, broken

by the horse named Custer's Revenge, I remember the Indian cowboy
rode a horse through a fence, after the bell, through four-by-six boards,
I remember the horse named Custer's Revenge broke through a fence,
I remember the Indian cowboy rode a horse named Custer's Revenge.

*

The United States Cavalry shot 1,000 ponies & only 1 survived,
she was found, someone found her, she was found in Montana,
giving birth to a colt, born running from the United States Cavalry,
born running into the Kentucky Derby, giving birth to a colt

named Spokane, the colt named Spokane running in the Kentucky Derby,
born running into the mile-and-a-half, from the United States Cavalry,
the colt named Spokane won the Kentucky Derby, set a record
for the mile-and-a-half, the colt named Spokane was born running.

*

My cousin rode his horse in a reservation cross-country race,
my cousin rode his horse to the top of Wellpinit Mountain,

28

my cousin was miles ahead of the nearest horse at the top
of the mountain, my cousin was miles ahead of the nearest horse

but his horse would not go down the mountain, my cousin whipped
the horse, kicked the horse bloody, but the horse would not go
down the mountain, my cousin cried and whipped, kicked the horse
bloody, but the horse would not, would not go down the mountain.

*

Last night, I woke to the sound of gunshots,
1,000 rifles, last night, I woke to the sound
of gunshots, 1,000 rifles, last night, I woke
to the sound of gunshots, 1,000 rifles, last night,
I woke to the sound of gunshots, 1,000 rifles,
last night, I woke to the sound of gunshots.

*

The Plains Indian rode her horse 18 hours a day, the Plains Indian
rode under her horse's neck into battle, the Plains Indian shot
seven arrows consecutively, the Plains Indian had seven arrows
in flight simultaneously, the Plains Indian rode her horse 18 hours a day.

There are witnesses.

*

After I heard the story on the radio,
the story I had never heard before,
I wanted to steal it all back, steal
1,000 ponies back from the United States Cavalry,

steal the ponies stolen from the Spokane Indians,
steal the horse named Spokane, steal
the Kentucky Derby, steal the mile-and-a-half,
steal every pony in my life.

*

My brother, the bingo caller, made five hundred in tips one week,
my brother went to the horse races, my brother bet five hundred dollars,

on the daily double, in the first race Grammas Luck won by a length,
my brother's horse won by a length in the first race, in the second,

my brother lost it all, in the second race Go Fast lost a photo finish,
my brother's horse lost a photo finish, my brother holding ten tickets,
ripping them into halves, my brother holding ten tickets, ripping them
into halves, my brother strangely in love with himself.

*

1,000 ponies shot
& only 1 survived.

*

The Indian was measured before
by the number of horses he owned,
the wealth of an Indian was determined
by the exact number of horses

he owned, I own no
horses, I own no horses,
my next door neighbors own
a dozen horses, my cousins

own more horses than I can count,
I own no horses,
the Indian was measured before
by the number of horses he owned,

the exact number, I own
no horses, I own
no horses, I own
no horses.

SONGS FROM THE FILM

Most movies are just sequels to my life.
— Chief Victor, Sr.

TRANSLATED FROM THE AMERICAN

after all the drive-in theaters have closed
for winter   I'll make camp alone
at THE NORTH CEDAR   replay westerns

the Seventh Cavalry riding double formation
endlessly   Main Avenue stretches
past the Union Gospel Mission   where I keep
a post office box   miles away

at my permanent address   I'll wrap myself
in old blankets   wait   for white boys
climbing fences   to watch this Indian speak

in subtitles   they'll surround me
and when they ask   "how"
I'll give them exact directions

CUSTER SPEAKS

My voice is for war!
— George Armstrong Custer, age seven

1.

I knew from the beginning. I was just seven years old
when I received my name but not by the same vision as the Indian, Crazy Horse
who starved himself for his. I was beautiful and large in town hat
and carved hair watching a military parade: all the shine, the fine men
with swords drawn and raised straight into the air, on horseback, pointing
the way toward heaven. I raised my arms above my head and shouted down
the entire world grown smaller and smaller beside the man I would become.

2.

Listen: every part of me is for battle, the charge, that perfect moment
        between fear and glory.
Sweet Jesus, don't you see? It all belonged to me, the Civil War
        was my war, the war to free
my soul. At Bull Run, I was first riding down the hill, leading
        young and old, holding
my saber. Goddamn, saber is a beautiful word. Saber, saber, saber.
        Nothing can be more beautiful
than leading thousands of men into the fight, carrying their lives
        on my shoulders
and when they fell, they fell beside me and I promise you
        I knew the name of every man.
That name was the same as mine. General George Armstrong Custer
        I remain, I remain.

3.

I see by your eyes what you think of me, of my surprise ride into
        Black Kettle's camp on the Washita River. It's easy
to blame me, to call it a massacre. But it was no Sand Creek, no
        Wounded Knee. Still, call me what you need to call me:
the Great Indian Fighter who cut down women and children, ordered
        them shot as they sought cover, shot them in the back.
But I was forced to do that. They attacked us with everything, everyone
        they had. It was maddening to see an Indian girl
pick up a rifle from the blood-soaked snow and fire at my men, at me.
        It doesn't change anything, make the fight mean less.

Just because Black Kettle's camp was on the reservation doesn't allow it
        to be called anything short of victory.
They had to be removed to make Kansas, the West, safe. They were barriers
        to progress. You call it genocide; I call it economics.

4.
If you want reasons or definitions, you can look at the history books.
If you want the truth, I will tell you exactly why I fell in love with all
those Blackfoot, Sioux, Crow. It was because they made a better hunt
than the buffalo ever did, but you must remember every drop of Indian blood
spilled was a political act, another building block toward the Presidency
the White House, all the headlines screaming my name in three inch print.
Please, in a time which required heroes, I was only a man.

5.
Crazy Horse, 0 my beautiful Crazy Horse. The first time I saw him
        he attacked my camp at the mouth
of the Tongue River. It's an ironic name for that dry and dusty place
        where Crazy Horse and I first stared across battle lines
eye to eye, heart to heart, but he didn't stand apart from the others.
        He was plain, a single feather in his hair, unpainted body
but I knew instantly who he was, he looked like me. Not in the physical way
        it was his presence that seemed to say
to shout his name across my chest. Crazy Horse and I were twins
        the best kind of men, the men who always win.
It was a revelation, almost Christ come back on horseback to chase
        a dark-skinned Lucifer across the plains, both of us
recreating the universe but he escaped me that day and every other day
        until I could only whisper his name in my sleep.

6.
Don't misunderstand the kind of man I really am.
If it was me, threatened by the loss of everything I had ever known
if it was me, frightened by the thought of being left alone
in a prison cell called the reservation, if it was me, I would go to hell
before I would give up the fight, the right to be free on the open plain.
I felt for their pain, their dreams, their lives.
Do you really think I could order the slaughter of 800 ponies and not cry?

7.
The last time I saw Crazy Horse, I rode my stallion, retreating
        at the Little Big Horn

that small and beautiful river where I was born. I rode
        to the top of a bluff
named after me now, to the top of Custer's Bluff, where he waited
        for me, Crazy Horse
my dear brother, and a thousand other warriors. I dismounted
        counted the number
of bullets and men I had left, and knew it was over. I cried
        and fought, shouted
the names of everyone I lost. I raised my arms straight up
        directly into the air
and watched a solitary man with long hair and blue eyes ride toward me
        alone, and then I was gone.

*

I was born again in Hiroshima.
I was born again in Birmingham.
I was born again in the Triangle Shirt Factory.
I was born again in Chile.
I was born again in Saigon.
I was born again in Iraq.
I was born again in Hollywood.

RESERVATION GRAFFITI

Robert Harris, where are you?

chickenbone in the throat reservation white boy dreamer
poor poor so poor the commodity Indians called you poor
YOU ARE HERE skinnyspit half-braid Indian boys beat you
flat earth pressed their ears against your empty stomach

heard this:

jazz hungry   one-fourth drum   the ice age

basketball on fire   hand grenades & horseshoes

song from the film   eyelashes   broken glass

reverberation

Robert Harris, where are you?

tied tight to the powwow fence Indian girls slapped your face
threw snowballs baseballs rocks woolly mammoths asphalt missiles
concrete bullets plastic arrows rubber hatchets razor treaties
spit in your mouth pissed on your shoes called you by your name

said this:

you don't belong
we know what white sounds like
it sounds
like horses drowning
like neon echoing
like flipping a light switch

Robert Harris, we are waiting.

our Indian mothers and fathers have cooked the last good meal
there is forgiveness in the fry bread confession in the chili
in every bar in Springdale we look at ourselves into our face
OBJECTS IN MIRROR ARE CLOSER THAN THEY APPEAR we love our sins

                    believe this:

              if you sit down beside me
                    I'll buy you
                        beer
                    slow laughter
              a hand on your back
           when we leave at closing time
                    together

Come back, come back, Robert Harris, there is no one left who remembers us,
remembers the children who set fire to their future and fancydanced easily.

POSTCARDS TO COLUMBUS

Beginning at the front door of the White House, travel west
for 500 years, pass through small towns and house fires, ignore
hitchhikers and stranded motorists, until you find yourself
back at the beginning of this journey, this history and country

folded over itself like a Mobius strip. Christopher Columbus
where have you been? Lost between Laramie and San Francisco
or in the reservation HUD house, building a better mousetrap?
Seymour saw you shooting free throws behind the Tribal School

in a thunderstorm. Didn't you know lightning strikes the earth
800 times a second? But, Columbus, how could you ever imagine
how often our lives change? *Electricity is lightning pretending
to be permanent* and when the Indian child pushes the paper clip

into the electrical outlet, it's applied science, insane economics
of supply and demand, the completion of a 20th century circuit.
Christopher Columbus, you are the most successful real estate agent
who ever lived, sold acres and acres of myth, a house built on stilts

above the river salmon travel by genetic memory. Beneath the burden
of 15,000 years my tribe celebrated this country's 200th birthday
by refusing to speak English and we'll honor the 500th anniversary
of your invasion, Columbus, by driving blindfolded cross-country

naming the first tree we destroy *America*. We'll make the first guardrail
we crash through our national symbol. Our flag will be a white sheet
stained with blood and piss. Columbus, can you hear me over white noise
of your television set? Can you hear ghosts of drums approaching?

WORTH WINNING

You're shooting pool with a stranger, a red-headed white man who shouldn't be here, shooting eight-ball at a dollar a game. Small time, but the red-headed white man keeps winning, never misses, and you know losing a dollar means losing a beer, and you're getting more sober and broke, but you're not the kind of Indian to wait outside and jump this red-headed white man, steal your money and his money. You're not even much of an Indian, you suppose, with your short hair and even teeth, but all the Skins in the bar are watching the red-headed white man beat your ass, and you know they'll take the money if you don't, they will probably kill this red-headed white man for a few dollars, so you have nothing and everything to lose, and after you give him your last dollar and he leaves, you follow him with a pool cue, and you're not the kind of Indian who would do this, but you follow him, thinking maybe you can call this your last stand.

POWWOW POLAROID

We were fancydancing, you see.

Step-step, right foot, step-step, left foot, faster, twisting, turning, spinning, changing.

There are photographs taken but only one ever captured the change. It was a white tourist from Spokane. She was lucky, she was quick, maybe it was film developed by the CIA.

She took the picture, the flashbulb burned, and none of us could move. I was frozen between steps, my right foot three inches off the ground, my mouth open and waiting to finish the last sound.

The crowd panicked. Most fled the stands, left the dancers not dancing and afraid. The white woman with the camera raised her arms in triumph, crossed her legs at the ankle, tilted her head to one side.

My four-hundred pound aunt wept into the public address system. My uncle held his great belly in his hands, walked among the fancydancers, said this:

forgiveness.

TEXAS CHAINSAW MASSACRE

What can you say about a movie so horrific
even its title scares people away?
— Stephen King

I
have seen it
and like it: The blood,
the way like *Sand Creek*
even its name brings fear,
because I am an American
Indian and have learned
words are another kind of violence.

This vocabulary is genetic.

When Leatherface crushes the white boy's skull
with a sledgehammer, brings it down again and again
while the boy's arms and legs spasm and kick wildly
against real and imagined enemies, I remember

another killing floor

in the slaughter yard from earlier in the film,
all the cows with their stunned eyes and mouths
waiting for the sledgehammer with fear so strong
it becomes a smell that won't allow escape. I remember

the killing grounds

of Sand Creek
where 105 Southern Cheyenne and Arapaho women and children
and 28 men were slaughtered by 700 heavily armed soldiers,
led by Colonel Chivington and his Volunteers. *Volunteers.*

Violence has no metaphors; it does have reveille.

Believe me, there is nothing surprising
about a dead body. This late in the 20th century

44

tears come easily and without sense:
taste and touch have been replaced
by the fear of reprisal. I have seen it

and like it: The butchery, its dark humor
that thin line "between art and exploitation,"
because I recognize the need to prove blood
against blood. I have been in places
where I understood *Tear his heart out*
and eat it whole. I have tasted rage
and bitterness like skin between my teeth.

I have been in love.

I first saw it in the reservation drive-in
and witnessed the collected history
of America roll and roll across the screen,
voices and dreams distorted by tin speakers.

"Since then, I have been hungry
for all those things I haven't seen."

This country demands that particular sort of weakness:
we must devour everything on our plates
and ask for more. Our mouths hinge open.
Our teeth grow long and we gnaw them down
to prevent their growth into the brain. I have

seen it and like it: The blood,
the way like music
it makes us all larger
and more responsible
for our sins,
because I am an American
Indian and have learned

hunger becomes madness easily.

ARIA

I acknowledge you, black man
who first loved the curve
of the buffalo.
I acknowledge you, buffalo woman
who stood still and loved
the black man back.

And I give thanks.

I give thanks to the whips
I give thanks to the chains
to the ships carrying my fathers from Africa.

I give thanks to the past
I give thanks to Buffalo Bill
to the greasy grass my mothers bled upon.

And I give thanks.

And I sing alone.

SUNDAYS, TOO

That was the summer all of us Indians drank the same brand of beer. At first, it was coincidence, economics. Then, it grew into a living thing, evolved and defined itself, became a ceremony, a tribal current, a shared synapse.

Often, it was beautiful: twenty or thirty Indians climbing out of a single reservation car like alcoholic circus clowns, all of us drinking the same brand of beer, half-cases half-full and tucked under arms. Our children loved us.

Standing in circles around fires, the Indians drank, laughed easily, laughed until the laughter was all. It was incestuous, moments so immediate, so familial, the air trembled because the Indians would not.

After hours of this drinking, only a few beers remained, the Indians shared, drank from the same can, bottle. Thick lips tasted and touched where other lips tasted and touched. It was communion, baptism, confession.

Later, in the dark, breathing replaced light as the source of our vision. Inside Bear, I saw the shape of her breath, distinct from the tiny storm Coyote created as he masturbated on the hood of the reservation car, separate from the hurried noise of Wolf pushing Raven against a pine tree, all of it coming together, sounding more and more like water meeting other water, like a small stone rolling down to strike a larger stone, rolling down to strike a boulder, bringing down a mountain.

There is nothing we cannot survive.

THE UNAUTHORIZED BIOGRAPHY
OF LESTER FALLSAPART

1.
Born on Christmas Day
& named _____

unpronounceable
in English & Indian

but it means *He Who Hunts*
With a Crooked Bow

& One Bad Arrow
Looking for Enough Deer

to Feed the Entire Tribe.
We just call him Lester.

2.
1979
in the dumpster reservation

behind the Trading Post.
Lester, is that you

shoved into a bottle
of Thunderbird Wine

piece by piece
like those hobby ships

we call minor miracles?
It takes years

to destroy yourself this way
without a reason to live

& not enough money
to buy a quick death.

3.
Stray dogs
sleep next to Lester

close
to whatever warmth

he has left.
I remember one mongrel

followed Lester all
over the reservation

as he collected
cans on roadsides.

The dog chased cars
half-crazed & half-exact.

That mutt is my cousin
Lester told us.

When the dog died
torn under a logging truck

Lester wept & refused to leave
his body in the ditch.

4.
The smallest pain
can change the world.

5.
1966
& the post office refused

to deliver Lester's mail
because he lived in a tipi

his life collected
in the dead letter box:

draft notice
postcards from Columbus

form letter
addressed incorrectly

to LESTER FELL APART.
Years later

as Lester pawned
his Purple Heart

he gave me that letter
& said

Somebody knew about my future
and tried to warn me.

Tell me, Lester
have you learned the best weapons

don't leave physical evidence?
In your mind

Viet Nam & the reservation
fancydance together.

6.
Unemployment checks
weigh more

than your own body
laid across the spine.

Lester, have you tried
to find work this week?

Nothing left
on the reservation

but buckets of dirty water
at the uranium mine

& Lester refuses
to carry that burden.

There are things I won't do
no matter how hungry I get

Lester tells me
as we travel into the trees

to cut a few cords
of firewood

for a flame
Lester will never feel.

Old women
pay Lester a few dollars

to carry groceries
from the Trading Post.

Old men
give Lester a shot

from their whiskey bottles
in a tribal gesture.

On warm nights
Lester sleeps

under a picnic table
in the BIA compound.

Sleeping outdoors
gives me strange dreams

Lester tells me
as we stop

next to the largest pine tree
on the reservation.

Then, Lester jumps
from the truck

raises my axe
above his head

looking to make
the first cut.

7.
Still, Lester sings
a good song & drums

like he could begin
this game again

roll the dice
pass GO

& collect his $200.
Day by day

he survives
this way.

CITIZEN KANE

How we are hungry for the word
to rise from our dark belly
past the throat and teeth,

one word

to change or not change
                              the world.
It doesn't matter which
as long as our failures are spectacular:

Big Mom lay on her cancer bed and cried out *Frybread*;
Lester slapped his drunk arms and legs and whispered *Snakes*;
Junior sold his blood for the 100th time and asked *Forgiveness*.

Believe me, nothing is forgotten for history.

Rosebud.

Believe me, nothing is innocent
when the camera rolls,
our sins are black and white.

Rosebud.

Listen: when the sun falls
audibly on the reservation
each of us choose the word
that determines our dreams:

whiskey   salmon   absence.

THE MARLON BRANDO
MEMORIAL SWIMMING POOL

There are no mistakes on the reservation, no flubbed lines or marks missed,
      no boom mike intruding
down into the frame for the audience to notice, spoiling every sense of
      realism, no irregularities
in time, space, or object. We've had a man in charge of continuity for 500
      years. If Lester FallsApart
holds a half-empty beer in his hand during a crucial scene then he'll still
      be holding a half-empty beer
in his hand during the second take, the third, until the director yells *Print
      that!* Dress rehearsals will
be formalities. Our sense of character will be methodical. You'll almost
      believe every Indian is an Indian.

*

I can't believe it. This late in the 20th century and Dennis Banks
      and Marlon Brando are eating
finger sandwiches out by the swimming pool. This must be fiction. But, wait,
      whatever happened to AIM?
Did they all drown because Marlon refused to pay for a lifeguard? *That's
      impossible*, Vine Deloria, Jr. says
there was never any water in the pool. In Okie's, I heard the story that
      Leonard Peltier left town
after a terrible performance in another reservation high school production
      of A STREETCAR NAMED DESIRE
but the Skin who told me that lie wore his hair in a weak braid, his whole
      life falling out of the knot.
Where is the news we can trust? Edward R. Murrow is lost in Beijing and CNN
      has finally lost its satellite link.
Last year, a local news crew filmed a softball game between the Spokane Tribe
      and a military team travelling in
from the local air force base. In the bottom of the ninth, down by three
      with the bases loaded, Seymour at bat
when he was hit by a fastball from the air force pitcher. One run scored.
      Lester up next and he got beaned
by a wicked slider, scoring another run. Chief Victor then stepped into the
      batter's box. Blasted by a thunderous pitch
he staggered to first while another Indian came home from third and tied
      the game. Junior came to the plate

with Seymour, the winning run, leading off third, and ran the count to full:
   two strikes, three balls.
The air force pitcher threw the change-up and Junior watched it all the way
   into the catcher's mitt. Imagine
Marlon Brando was the umpire. Would he call it a ball or a strike? Imagine
   Dennis Banks as the first
Native American real estate agent, selling a 5,000 gallon capacity dream
   in the middle of a desert.
Imagine the dream is cracked, leaks into the surrounding sand, wastes so
   much time and money. Imagine Banks
trades the pool for everything west of the Mississippi. Imagine Banks sold
   the pool to *Some white guy*.
Imagine he sold it to Cotton Mather. Imagine he sold it to Andrew Jackson.
   Imagine the want ads
fancydancing through the newspapers. Imagine Marlon Brando dressed up like
   an Indian for the commercials
on late night television. Imagine the possibilities. Imagine Coyote accepts
   the Oscar for lifetime achievement.
Imagine the Marlon Brando Memorial Swimming Pool as monument to war,
   to the insane economics of supply and demand.
Imagine the reservation metaphors: no water in the pool and it's like my
   stomach; pour whiskey into the pool
until it smells like my kidney; fill it with salt water and add a few sharks;
   throw a bag full of kittens
or Indians into the deep end. Imagine the possibilities. Imagine the songs.
   Imagine how our lives will change.

*

There are no mistakes on the reservation. The 20th century warrior relies
   on HBO for his vision
at three in the morning. Last night, it was THE GODFATHER made me realize
   how a slight gesture
can change the world, how the smallest facial tic can give the illusion of
   perfection, by highlighting
imperfection. Marlon Brando, cheap diamond, lisping genius, why did you
   slow dance with Dennis Banks
beside the swimming pool of every Indian's dreams? Why do you hide so often
   on your own private island
that personal reservation in the Pacific? All these years later, Marlon,
   and you on live television
defending your son, Christian, against murder charges. Do you remember
   Leonard Peltier? Do you remember

he stood at the window of the farm house in South Dakota yelling *Stella!*
        Stella! while the FBI surrounded him
and the rest of AIM, a cast of thousands. It was epic, a Cecil B. DeMille
        production made intimate
when two FBI agents were shot to death. The murder weapon was a rifle Peltier
        never touched, a rifle
Dennis Banks never touched, a rifle Marlon Brando never touched, but
        they were all guilty
of some crime or another, all wore their braids tucked under a black hat,
        all fancydanced away
from the fire and went home alone. Peltier goes blind in Leavenworth, Banks
        rents limousines in Rapid City
and Brando sits, fat and naked, by the Pacific ocean. *There was never any*
        water in the damn thing,
Vine Deloria tells me again and I believe him because the Marlon Brando
        Memorial Swimming Pool waits
for a buyer, another dreamer who will imagine the pool is filled with water,
        with bingo cards, with uranium
just beginning a half-life, with the very last salmon, with every Urban Indian
        looking to find a way home.

HOSPITAL FOOD

All day I have been waiting for the first sandwich in the lunch of dreams. There is a nurse wearing red shoes who brings me ice cream in the middle of the night, feeds me like a child. "Son," she whispers. "The elevator doors of the future are closing tight on your foot." Often she will sing to me, teach me the lyrics of obscure show tunes. "Nurse," I asked one night. "Do you want to learn the songs I know? The songs of horses exploding, broken glass, light breaking through used coffee filters, and empty paper bags?" She leaned over me and whispered, "Young Indian boy, you are stumbling off the escalator of desire." In the bed next to me in the semi-private room paid for by the BIA, a sixteen-year-old white boy with a bad heart. He sleeps under the oxygen tent at night. His parents have become afraid of him, send him postcards from San Francisco, Disneyland, Sea World. They sent him a MONOPOLY game and we play until he runs out of breath. "It's the money," he says. "The money is too damn heavy." At night I lay awake listening to his breathing, measure it against mine. Some nights I stand over him, stare down through the clear plastic of his tent. "This is your temporary atmosphere," I whisper to him. "Your body is lying to itself 45 times a minute." Every breath is a treaty. One night I crawled under the sheets with him, placed my dark hand on his pale, scarred chest. His heartbeat felt like coins dropping into a collection plate. "Young white boy," I whispered. "When you are gone, I will need your steel-toed boots." His breath slowed, his eyes opened, and he said, "I understand your needs, but it is too late. Your right foot is bleeding profusely."

SNAPPING THE FRINGE

She was there before the camas root grew jealous of the power of her hair, after I tasted her in the fry bread.

That full-blood beauty never wore braids.

She was the fancydancer who didn't speak English on any reservation; she wore her shawl like a bright red promise, snapping the fringe.

She keeps you awake, leaves you sitting all night long in the video game hall with the powwow refuse, gives you nothing to do but eat Indian tacos with too much commodity cheese.

At three in the morning there are no locked doors on the powwow grounds. I creep among the tipis, the breathing of so many Indians like a long and slow song.

In the distance insomniac children break glass against their braids, their easy laughter leaping into the air, shifting from pine tree to pine tree.

A Coeur d'Alene Indian whistles from the bottom of a mud puddle.

A Spokane Indian cracks his knuckles inside a rainwater-filled tin can.

Then, she is there fancydancing in the dust of the rodeo grounds, in a circle of headlights, all the reservation cars beating their horns like
drums?

Now, during the Last Goodbye Dance, the drummers look deep into the circle of dancers dancing around them. They recognize her dark eyes.

The old Indian men in flannel, in blue parkas, sitting in the front row, hold their breath as she dances by, snapping the fringe an inch from their faces.

Sometimes, she draws blood.

That full-blood beauty doesn't need to wear buckskin. The deer sleep uneasily among the trees, dreaming of the power of her touch, of the way she can cover you, good and warm.

SONGS FROM THE FILM

John B. drove the getaway car in one of those black and white movies the reservation theater played years before it was filmed.

John B. was in the driver's seat of the '57 Chevy, whistling the last song the Spokane Indians invented, his fingers snapping the first song across their own bones.

It happens that way: the body will not forget the rhythm of survival. Drums, drums, drums.

John B. listened to his AM radio, the reservation station all-request hour. He sang along to every song, knew the face of every Indian voice dreaming out loud.

Come with me, wild and free, to the sea, the sea of love

John B. closed his eyes and all over the reservation there was the music of commodity cans, of dark skin moving over dark skin, of children throwing rocks through windows, of the BIA truck turning a sharp corner, of the skinny dog screaming in the dark, of memory repeating itself like a scratched record.

You will be mine, you will be mine, all mine
You will be mine, you will be mine, all mine

In the bars, fancydancers change their minds, jump on the pool tables and tear up the felt with their large shoes.

In the cities, Indian boys pull at their crew cuts until black hair catches fire and grows longer with every change of pitch in the wind.

In the trees, songs dance from pine to pine, from HUD house to HUD house, from wood stove to microwave.

This one is dedicated to all of us: John B. was driving down the longest highway in tribal history when he took his hands off the wheel.

He was the first and last Skin to leave the road.

CRAZY HORSE SPEAKS

1.
I discovered the evidence
in a vault of The Mormon Church
3,000 skeletons of my cousins
in a silence so great
I built four walls around it
and gave it a name.
I called it Custer
and he came to me
again in a dream.
He forgave all my sins.

2.
Little Big Horn.
Little Big Horn does not belong to me.
I was there
my horse exploded beneath me.
I searched for Long Hair
the man you call Custer
the man I call My Father.
But it wasn't me who killed him
it was _____
who poked holes in Custer's ears
and left the body for proof.
I dream of him
and search doorways and alleys
for his grave.
General George Armstrong Custer
my heart is beating
survive   survive   survive.

3.
I wear the color of my skin
like a brown paper bag
wrapped around a bottle.
Sleeping between
the pages of dictionaries
your language cuts
tears holes in my tongue

61

until I do not have strength
to use the word *Love*.
What could it mean
in this city where everyone is
Afraid-of-Horses?

4.

There are places I cannot leave.
Rooms without doors or windows
the eternal ribcage.
I sat across the fire
from Sitting Bull
shared smoke and eyes.
We both saw the same thing
our futures tight and small
an 8 x 10 dream
called the reservation.
We had no alternatives
but to fight again and again
live our lives on horseback.
After the Civil War
the number of Indian warriors
in the West doubled
tripled the number of soldiers
but Indians never have shared
the exact skin
never the same home.

5.

I am the mirror
practicing masks
and definitions.
I have always wanted to be anonymous
instead of the crazy skin
who rode his horse backward
and laid down alone.
It was never easy
to be frightened
by the sound of a color.
I can still hear white
it is the sound
of glass shattering.

6.
I hear the verdict
in the museum in New York
where five Eskimo were flown in
to be a living exhibit.
Three died within days
lacking natural immunity
their hearts miles
and miles of thin ice.
The three dead Eskimo
were stuffed and mounted
hunched over a fishing hole
next to the two living
who held their thin hands
close to their chests
mortal and sinless.

7.
Whenever it all begins again
I will be waiting.

DROUGHT

So many old Indians stopped drinking
just one drink before the drink
which would have killed them..

I'll write poetry exactly that way.
— Seymour

RESERVATION STEW

1 pound venison
2 cups carrots, sliced
2 cups potatoes, diced
2 cups celery, chopped
1 large onion, minced
1 bay leaf
thyme
salt & pepper to taste

The Indian mother places her life on the cutting board. She has been waiting for years, her hips heavy with memories of children dead by housefire and car-wreck, children lost to college and prison, children abandoned by fathers and rent due, children born to children. She wants them all back.

Years ago, there was enough for everyone.

Now, the Indian mother measures every emotion exactly. A moment of sadness can be wasted easily. She finds leftovers from years of dreaming will not feed even the smallest heart.

In the grocery store, she digs into her change purse, needing a quarter for carrots, but finds a note instead: *Sorry. I needed the money for cigarettes.*

The Indian mother walks into the hills, followed by generations of need. Can this pine tree substitute for a pickup truck? Do the small stones taste anything like hard candy? Will the bank accept deer tracks as collateral toward a home loan?

The Indian mother is afraid; she is not afraid.

At night, she sits by the window and watches for her children. Sometimes, they are bats flapping at streetlights or stray dogs howling in the dark. Once, her oldest son dressed up like a bear and slept on the roof of the Catholic church.

The Indian mother sings while she cooks, in a voice sharp enough to pull roots from the ground. She pours her whole life, her children, her children's children into the stew pot and simmers all over open flame.

After years of this slow cooking, she still waits to serve the last good meal.

CRISIS ON TOAST

We've been driving for hours
my father and I
through reservation farmland
talking the old stories:
Stubby Ford; Lana Turner
at the National Boy Scout Jamboree
my father pissing in a hole he dug
while his troop formed a circle
around him and Lana Turner drove by
breaking every boy's heart. He told me

old drunk stories
about the gallon of vodka a day
the DTs, snakes
falling out of the walls. We watched

two farm boys shooting baskets. Lean and hungry
they were "suicidally beautiful." *Jesus*
my father said. *I played ball like that*.
I looked into the sun and tears fell
without shame or honor. We got out of the car
in our basketball shoes. My father's belly
two hundred winter beers wide
and I've never been more afraid
of the fear in any man's eyes.

POEM FOR JAMES WHO ASKED ME WHY
EVERYTHING HURTS SO MUCH

My own days bring me slaps on the face.
— Lorna Dee Cervantes

. . . and his eyes were furtive, wild,
as if he'd already seen
too much.
— Jay Griswold

Today, it's too warm to see winter
approaching: the wasps are more important
than vision. The BIA seeded 100 queens
onto the reservation to kill aphids

and *we shouldn't eliminate their nests*
unless it's absolutely necessary.
My little brother stood at the front door
and raged against the sexless wasps

that battered at the screen. Ten years of age
even his days bring slaps to his face.
For revenge, he half-filled a glass gallon jar
with water, set a few marshmallows to float as bait

and punched a hole in the lid large enough
for a wasp to enter. I watched him build
his death machine and watched him watching
the wasps struggle against water and drown.

Look, he said. *One of those wasps is using another one*
like a raft. It's true: I stood beside my brother
as one wasp flipped another beneath the surface
and climbed onto its back. We all want to survive.

Look, my brother said and it was not beautiful
nor cruel. It was an ornamental medicine
because there was nothing left to heal.
It was the smallest possible war and still

                              too large.

THE 35TH ANNUAL YAKIMA NATION ALL-INDIAN BASKETBALL TOURNAMENT

1.
I can't believe it—
the 20th century arrived

moments before the clock started
on the all-Indian basketball game

when a braided man sang
THE STAR SPANGLED BANNER

accompanied by drum
and a strange sun

breaking through windows.
A crazy woman

from Hollywood
or Montana

photographed Skins
announced over the PA system

she's a scout
for a major motion picture studio

casting extras for the remake
of LAST OF THE MOHICANS.

She surrounded us
in the visitor's locker room

asked Piapot
What kind of cars do Indians drive?

He told her to walk outside
and look in the parking lot.

Sweetheart, history
doesn't always look like horses.

2.
Indians from everywhere
drinking beer

in a nameless bar
when Junior suggests

we should buy a case to go
and drive to Yakima

and we all agree
until someone reminds us

we're already in Yakima.
It happens that way:

> our body forgets
> the rhythm of survival.

3.
Here, my father
told us the story

of the white cop
who stopped him

stole his shoes
and gave him five minutes

to run the last mile
across the reservation border.

> God bless you, America
> my father is still running.

4.
3 a.m. and Seymour
screws an Indian girl

in the motel bathroom
while I pretend to sleep

some tribe or another
powwows by the ice machine

and the graveyard shift manager
threatens to call the police

    everybody singing
    I love you, I love you.

5.
Breakfast
in the House of Pancakes

and the white waitress
ignores my empty

coffee cup.
I leave her

    a dollar bill
    folded into a question mark.

SPOKANE, 1976

How easy to be Indian
in the Park Lane Motel.

From the bathroom window
I could see K Mart
if I stood on the toilet.

Dad had money in his wallet
and four kids small enough
to all sleep in the same bed
while he and Mom lay down together on the floor.

We watched karate movies
at the East Sprague Drive-In
and I didn't mind the dubbed dialogue.

It would be years before my voice was lost the same way.

Mornings, we'd catch a bus downtown
and I browsed through old comic books
at Dutch's Pawn Shop and never worried
about the televisions, typewriters, guitars.

Then, Dutch's musty smell was like a secret guarded.
I didn't know it was quiet desperation.

How wonderful my father knew every drunk Indian in the city!

Once, my father gave five dollars
to a Skin with a nose so bruised
I could not see his eyes.

It might have been God.

Once, my father saw an old Indian
man weeping on the corner and drove around the block twelve times
before he remembered the old man's name
and shouted it out the window so the old man would also remember.

That was the summer of continual fireworks.

Over Spokane Falls
in a blue gondola, I leaned over the edge
and saw ghosts of salmon jumping.

It was the kind of celebration this country would never see again.

SEATTLE, 1987

This late in the 20th century
I cannot look at a lake
without wondering what's beneath it:

drowned horses   snapping turtles   cities of protected bones.

Yesterday, the sun rose
so quickly on cable television
I thought it a new day   beginning
but it was just another camera trick.

How the heart changes
when this city fills with strange animals
the reservation never predicted

animals formed by the absence of song.

Downtown today, a street magician
so clumsy I fell in love
and threw a dollar bill into his top hat.

There are so many illusions I need to believe.

DROUGHT

Today, I walked with you
through streets of this city
where I spent so many years
of my life, poor, hungry, always
                              amazed.

Believe me: I was born from thirst
into thirst until I learned to love
                              my thirst.

So many Indians born with the alcohol spirit
and I'm no different. My heart still
staggers when I feel the next drink
                              touch my lips.

There is a reservation for every prisoner
willing to accept their four walls and window.

I remember the green walls and impossible window
of the tribal jail, that reservation
within a reservation, where my father waited
hours for a tin cup full of ice water
and drank it slowly, with pain and pleasure,
like it was his first and last drink
of the vodka which stole his dreams
                              without scent.

I have tried to give you a simple music
but you insisted on following me down
deeper into the wells until you touched what was left
of my dreams, of my insane thirst growing
                              without measure.

Sometimes, my friend, I am suddenly empty
without hope of rain.

Once, i wrote of dreaming of a country
where three inches of rain fell in an entire year.

Then, I believed it was a way
of measuring loss. Now, I believe
it was a way of measuring how much

we need to gain.

POEM

I lower a frayed rope into the depths
and hoist the same old Indian tears to my eyes.
The liquid is pure and irresistible.
— Adrian C. Louis

Could this be like the Trail of Tears
I ask myself, as I crawl inside
the Breakaway Bar, a trail of beers

marking my path like a clumsy deer
stumbling and unable to hide
from hunters on a trail of tears.

You can always find me mumbling here
about how I wounded my knee, pie-eyed
and falling on a trail of beers

picking up scars like roadside souvenirs.
Commodities can keep me pacified
now, on this two-lane trail of tears.

Cashing government checks like a premier
I'm an alcoholic Jekyll and Hyde
in tattered coat, on a trail of beers

giving my last twenty to the cashier
for another case, trying to decide
if I'm crawling along a trail of tears
or drowning myself on a trail of beers.

THE LAST INDIAN BAR IN SPOKANE

next to the porno shop
on Second Avenue, promised
to stay open until dawn

the last night it was open.
The jukebox played
Country & Western because

"Indians make the best cowboys."
Every time someone finished
a beer, he threw the empty across

the room, above Lester FallsApart
two-stepping with Suzy Boyd.
In those moments between

a glass thrown and a glass
shattering against the corner, promises
were everything

held tight in the fists:
dollar bills, beer bottles
hips, all meant the same thing

at dawn. The Skins rolled
out, stopped early
traffic. Fancydancing to car horns

and "Get your asses off the road"
it was six in the morning
it was last call for anything.

"SINNERS IN THE HANDS OF AN ANGRY GOD"

she, who once was my sister
dead in the house fire
now lying still in the coffin
her hair cut short
by an undertaker who never knew
she called her hair "Wild Ponies"

I don't know any beautiful words
for death or the reason why
sinners curl like blackened leaves
in the hands of God

she, who once was my sister
is now the dust
the soft edge of the earth

LETTER: A DEFINITION OF LOVE

for Leonard

"Look," it sez. "I never danced
for no damn rain beside the Grand Canyon
while some family from Ohio took
my picture and called me strong
in the sun. I just painted

and if my work was sold
for less than what it was worth
it was because I needed money
for food or rent. I didn't use my own blood

or spit to paint the stuff.
I bought it for two bucks a tube
downtown. I didn't pass out

in doorways, piss my pants drying out
and thin in some county jail.
I drank my beers alone
and went home alone. I don't have no scars

except scars from the car
that ran my ass over
in the dark near Vegas. I painted

a self-portrait in the hospital.
I colored the tubes, casts
nurses and doctors bone white
and burned it when I got out.
I called it *Love*
that's what I know."

RAIN

I learned to dream by watching the dog dream in his sleep, until he died and left me to dream all by myself.

In 1966, I imagined myself born with a thirst so large the rain stopped outside and started again in my skull.

Then, it is 1991 and John and I drive through reservation farmland and a summer storm, heat lightning and rain so hard we can't see through the windshield.

But to my right, the sun breaks through black clouds, a circle of light so perfect I want to be there now, standing in some anonymous field, finally a Child of the Sun.

John, I say. *I want to find that place, but it must be miles away.*

Junior, he tells me. *It's closer than you think.*

BREAKING OUT THE SHOVEL

Sometimes it is better not to know
How far the digging needs to go
Or if someone will come out and help
— Alex Kuo

Beginning somewhere near the reservation
I took shovel in hand and dug, expected

no help with the geography and distance
between first slice into earth and the last.

How the need to believe the childhood story
of digging all the way to China forced my hand

to shovel, heart to a terrible dream. Friend,
I was amazed to rise from 500 years of digging

to find you halfway across your own dreams,
shovel in your hand, digging from Beijing

straight down through the globe, never knowing
exactly where you would surface next:

in Buenos Aires; at Forbes Field leaning
over the rail to grab Clemente's last foul tip;

at a battered piano stunned by the *Goldberg Variations*.
How was I to know drums were never enough

music to fill the silence of children left
and dreams put quietly to bed?

Friend, this is a strange journey, digging
for hours, then days, through generations of need

and it is better not to know how much farther
the digging needs to go, but I want you to know

I often stop for rest, ask directions,
gauge distance and how much I need help

with this digging, this life, measured
meter by meter. I move through history

and my story and your story, gathering
into our warmth, this heart changing by halves.

1979

for Steve

If you hear the radio playing out my door, stop, listen, come in and visit.

We can drink old coffee, a beer, eat fry bread with too much butter. Tonight our excesses will be forgiven.

You and I can talk and laugh, remember the old stories, the old people we only remember when you and I talk together.

We can lie about the length of our braids, lie about all the Indian women we danced with at the last powwow.

I wasn't even at the last powwow, but you don't know that for sure. You weren't there, either.

It gets cold at night sooner in the year when I live off the reservation. I build fires in September.

If you hear the radio playing out my door, come in and we'll sit together. We'll watch the air between us. We'll smile at the sound of our breathing.

RED BLUES

Mom always said life with a poet would be rough.
— K. L. Cederblom

1.
Music. Then, more music. Does it matter what kind? Let's say it is bagpipes.
Or a grade school orchestra practicing *Roll on, Columbia, Roll on*. Or the blues.
Or just a drum that sounds like the blues. I have heard that kind of drum at three
in the morning when I pull myself from bed and my ordinary nightmares. Listen.

2.
Listen, listen, the cat is pissing. Where? Where? On the chair. Where's the chair?
Cousin, that chair is three-legged and dangerous. Place it at the inherited
piano and you'll fall when you reach for the farthest chord. It happens that
way. A white woman loves you so much that seeds fall from the cuffs of your
pants and grow into orange trees. She tells you *Don't ever underestimate the
importance of Vitamin C*, but she meant to say *Don't want everything so much*.

3.
So much to say tonight but the only payphone on the reservation is OUT OF
ORDER. Last week, I tried to call and two teenage Indian girls sent their dogs
after me when I told them I needed the phone. Once, an operator put me on
hold and left me there, halfway between touching and becoming. I didn't
have enough strength or quarters left to hang up. Then, your voice. Your
voice, again. Or is it just neon beer signs buzzing outside the Trading Post?
Or is it a car thumping over a cattle guard? Or is it this silence so brilliant I
can hear my deaf father's television from a mile away?

4.
The television was always too loud, until every conversation was distorted,
fragmented. *Come out with your hands up* sounded like *You will never have a
dream come true. The aliens are coming! The aliens are coming!* sounded like *Just
one more beer, sweetheart, and then we'll go home. I love you* sounded like *You've
got so much to lose.*

5.
I lost my wallet outside the 7–11 that summer and all I worried about was my
photograph of you. My last twenty dollar bill, social security card, driver's
license, tribal I.D., could never be introduced as evidence. I spent hours
digging through the dumpster but there was nothing.

6.
There is nothing as white as the white girl an Indian boy loves.

7.
Indian boy, can you hear that music? Then, more music? No, it's only a pebble rolling down to strike a small stone, rolling down to strike a larger stone, rolling down to strike a boulder, bringing down a mountain. This late in the 20th century, we still make the unknown ours by destroying it. There is nothing strange about a dead body or a lumber mill. I read in the newspaper that motorists kill over a thousand deer a year on the fifteen mile stretch of highway between Colville and Chewelah. No one wrote a letter to the editor. Now, I think of her white hands, how dissonant they look against my brown skin, how together we can easily destroy our worlds.

8.
Spin the globe, faster and faster, revolution after revolution, until you stop it with a fingertip. Where are you now? YOU ARE HERE. Nothing has changed. Black Elk said *Everything tries to be round*. Van Gogh said *Life is probably round*. We're all just trying to find our way back home.

9.
Touch home. I'm driving my car up the switchbacks so familiar I close my eyes. *Touch home*. Your hands on that piano almost too large for the room. *Touch home*. My best friend passed out next to the dumpster outside the Trading Post. *Touch home*. Your house older than the trees that surround it. *Touch home*. Blue Creek, Turtle Lake, so close to our uranium mine the water drives a Geiger counter crazy. *Touch home*. Your mirrors that don't hold my reflection. *Touch home*. My family portraits that don't carry a white face. *Touch home*. We don't have keys for the same doors.

10.
The door opens and closes again quickly. I hear the lock click. I knock at midnight, miles from my reservation and years from forgiveness. What can I tell you? What treaties can I sign now? *I'd hold you to all your promises if I could find just one I knew you'd keep*. America, I can see you outside my window, just beyond my doorstep, fading past the battered lawn. America, I hear your voice, your song every night before I fall asleep, *at the end of another broadcasting day*. America, I played Little League baseball. But I should have learned to dance. America, I have memorized the Pledge of Allegiance. But I should have learned to dance. America, I know the capitals of all fifty states. But I should have learned to dance. America, I follow your footprints, glowing in the dark. I followed them through grass, up walls and across ceilings. But I should have learned to dance.

11.
During the owldance, the woman asks the man to dance. If he refuses, he must pay the woman what she wishes and he must also stand before the entire crowd and tell them why he refused. Let's change the rules, reverse the world for a moment: *Will you dance with me?*

12.
Hello, you. Hello, me. Can you hear the music, Indian boy? Maybe it's a car radio. Maybe it's Bill Ford's Chevy cruising past the house. He's got just enough gas money to always be in the car. *Hello people we used to be.* Can you feel that bass, Indian boy, that treble and tremble? Maybe it's the last song at the reservation high school dance. Maybe it's the lead singer with braids who doesn't know how to read. He never learned to play guitar. *Isn't it strange? We never changed. We've been through it all yet we're still the same.* Can you recognize the tune, Indian boy, can you hum a few bars? Maybe it's that song you heard in the middle of the night years ago. Maybe you were half-asleep and thought it was the most beautiful song you ever heard. Maybe it was drums. *And I know it's a miracle that we still go, for all we know, we might still have a way to go.* Can you hear that voice, Indian boy, like an echo, like a divining rod? Maybe it's a *Rock and Roll Fantasy.* Maybe it's a summer flood rushing down the hill toward your future. Maybe it was the blues.

13.
Robert Johnson, Robert Johnson, where is that missing song? Someone told me it was hidden at Sand Creek. Someone told me it was buried near Wounded Knee. Someone told me Crazy Horse never died; he just picked up a slide guitar. Here I am, in the reservation of my mind and I don't even have a drum.

14.
If you listen close, if you listen tight, you can hear drums 24 hours a day. Someone told me once that a drum means *I love you;* someone told me later it means *Tradition is repetition.* Late at night, I take inventory of what I have lost, make plans for the future, but there's only so much I know about survival. The television is white noise and the midnight movie is just another western where the Indians lose. Nothing changes. So, I keep counting, *one little, two little, three little Indians,* all the way up to ten little Indian boys, stop, then start again, until I count the entire world. These small measurements are all I have as defense against inertia. Believe me, I can never call the reservation home. I don't have keys to any doors here; *I never learned to dance.* Listen, sweetheart. Can you hear that music? Then, more music? It's just me and my blues.

INDIAN SUMMER

It was the summer of grasshoppers
and *Sleep, sleep*
all my father could say
was *Sleep, sleep.*

The ponies couldn't run down by the church
their tongues licked and licked
                    the air.

My brother told me *They're catching salt*
but I didn't believe him, wouldn't believe
ever since he said the sun could change its mind

and I woke up early for a week, still in the dark
and watched the sun rise from the west
                         constantly.

It was the summer of battered grass
and empty taps. NO WATER, NO WATER
except in the uranium river
where Billy Nomad broke his neck diving
                         into the shallows.

The old school caught fire
and no one noticed
until it jumped from brick to pine
from pine to pine, from pine to skin.

My hair bled ash.

It was the summer of the continual powwow
and Ernie Game never wore a shirt or socks
but still managed enough gas money
                    to get back home.

Some Skin was always bouncing a basketball
over pavement, against ceiling and walls.
Once, I followed the sound, triangulated position
but could never find its source.

There have been smaller mysteries.

It was the summer of unbraided hair
and *Hush now! you ask too many questions*
when I wondered why Indians always die
by threes.

One, like a divining rod bent down to the ground.
Two, like a quilt imperfectly patched.
Three, like the sky folding over its horizon.

SHOES

I know there is something larger
than the memory of a dispossessed people. We have seen it.
—Joy Harjo

Let's say.
Let's say he was walking down the reservation road.
Let's say he was walking down the reservation road with no shoes and he's
        drunk.
Let's say he was walking down the reservation road with no shoes and he's
        drunk and it's three in the morning
and the pickup truck with no headlights hits him hard, lifts him into the
        air, carries him over the pine trees and HUD houses,
knocks his head against the big dipper, scrapes his feet on the bright moon,
        blackens his eyes with a night cloud,
throws him clear across the Spokane River until he's lying still in the
        grass, listening to his own body cool, waiting
for that first bold insect to come along and claim a piece of his flesh.

Let's say he gets broken down piece by piece.
Let's say he gets broken down piece by piece and somebody finds the body.
Let's say he gets broken down piece by piece and somebody finds the body,
        and makes it into another roadside attraction
and tourists on cross-country drives can stop in, look under the big tent
        and see the entire freak show, the oddity zoo:
"Ladies and gentlemen, come and see Jo Jo the Dog-Faced Boy, wonder at the
        strange gifts a human can be given, come see the Fat Lady,
the Bearded Woman, come see midgets and dwarves, come see the Snake Boy,
        come see the Man with Four Legs, wonder at the abominations
God has placed upon the earth, come see the Indian boy who was hit-and-run
        and rotted in the roadside grass for a week
before anyone bothered to stop their goddamned car and check his pulse."

How do you explain it?
How do you explain the survival of all of us who were never meant to survive?
How do you explain Bobby Sherwood, reservation pinball champion, 1974,
        dead in a car wreck on Ford Canyon Road that same year?
How do you explain Michael Sherwood, Bobby's brother, 250 pound offensive
        lineman, dead in a car wreck on Ford Canyon Road in 1986?

How do you explain Tony Sherwood, Mike and Bobby's brother, soon-to-be-
      Marine, hit-and-run, dead in the grass beside Ford Canyon Road?
How do you explain it?

I'm waiting.
I'm waiting for someone to tell the truth.
I'm waiting for the clap-trap, backtrack, flimflam, Viet Nam, fried Spam,
      Green Eggs and Ham, Grand Coulee Dam, sacrificial lamb.
I'm waiting for the big time, lemon-lime, mountain climb, uranium mine, orange
      rind, *the tumor's benign*, capital crime.
I'm waiting for the football team, sugar and cream, blue jeans, cross beam,
      95% lean, enlarged spleen, 24-hour wet dream.
I'm waiting for the fry bread, hydrocephalic head, U. S. government bed,
      underfed, unhappily wed, sandwich spread.
I'm waiting for the Christmas Day, hairspray, breakaway, Chevrolet, Cassius
      Clay, Milky Way, photoplay.

I'm waiting.
I'm waiting for a new kind of shoes.
I'm waiting for a new kind of shoes that can cover your mouth, can cover
      manholes and Grand Canyons, can walk over bridges and broken insects,
can tapdance on skulls and kitchen tile, shuffle over sand and diamonds,
      stomp on grass and briefcases, tiptoe through minefields and bedrooms.

I'm waiting.
I'm waiting for a better pair of shoes.
I'm waiting for a better pair of shoes than I got now, no more basketball
      shoes, no more dress shoes, no more Jesus shoes, no more *Damn
these are comfortable* shoes, no more high-heeled shoes, no more red shoes,
      no more blue shoes, no more black shoes, no more green shoes,
no more, no more, no more, no more, no more, no more, no more, no more shoes.

Do you remember?
Do you remember when you were a baby sticking your bare feet into your mouth,
      sucking on your own toes?
Do you remember all that simple joy?

ABOUT THE AUTHOR

Born in 1966, Sherman Alexie is an enrolled Spokane/Coeur d'Alene Indian from Wellpinit, Washington, on the Spokane Indian Reservation. Winner of a 1991 Washington State Arts Commission poetry fellowship and a 1992 National Endowment for the Arts poetry fellowship, Sherman Alexie has published more than two hundred poems, stories, and translations in *Another Chicago Magazine, Beloit Poetry Journal, Black Bear Review, Caliban, Journal of Ethnic Studies, Hanging Loose, New York Quarterly, Red Dirt, Slipstream, ZYZZYVA*, and others. His first book of poetry and short stories, *The Business of Fancydancing*, was published by Hanging Loose Press in January 1992, and his second collection, *I Would Steal Horses*, was the winner of *Slipstream*'s fifth annual Chapbook Contest in March 1992. He currently lives and works in Spokane, Washington.

ILLUSTRATOR

Poet and artist Elizabeth Woody, an enrolled member of the Confederated Tribes of Warm Springs, Oregon, attended the Institute of American Indian Arts in Santa Fe, New Mexico. She received a Brandywine Workshop Artist Fellowship for offset lithography, and her prints toured in a show entitled "Native Proof." In 1988, she was a recipient of an American Book Award from the Before Columbus Foundation for her first collection of poetry, *Hand into Stone.* Currently she lives in Portland, Oregon.